242.8.

**Leabharlanna Poiblí Chathair Bhaile Átha Cliath
Dublin City Public Libraries**

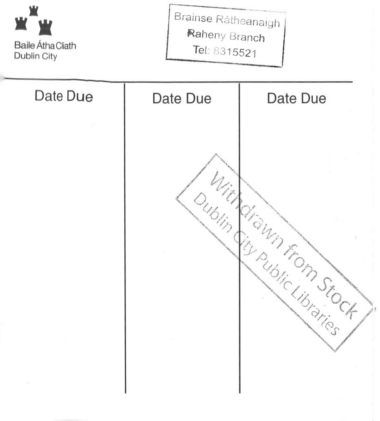

Baile Átha Cliath
Dublin City

Brainse Rátheanaigh
Raheny Branch
Tel: 8315521

| Date Due | Date Due | Date Due |
| --- | --- | --- |
| | | |

# A TREASURY OF PRAYERS

Dedicated to the Blessed Trinity,
Father, Son and Holy Spirit.


'I will restore to you the years
which the locust has eaten.'
*Joel 2:25*

Dinah Proctor

# A Treasury of Prayers

the columba press

First published in 2015 by
## the columba press
55A Spruce Avenue,
Stillorgan Industrial Park,
Blackrock, Co. Dublin


Cover design by David Mc Namara
Origination by The Columba Press
Printed by ScandBook AB, Sweden


ISBN 978 1 78218 231 3

Scripture Verses from the Jerusalem Bible
and the Good News Bible.

# Contents

# *Ordinary Prayers*

THE SIGN OF THE CROSS
In the name of the Father and the Son and the Holy Spirit. Amen.

THE CONFITEOR
I confess to Almighty God that I have sinned through my own fault, in my thoughts and in my words, in what I have done and in what I have failed to do, and I ask the Blessed Mary ever virgin, and all the Angels and Saints to pray for me to the Lord Our God.

ACT OF CONTRITION
O my God, I am heartily sorry for having offended thee and I detest my sins most sincerely because they displease thee O my God who are so deserving of all my love, for thy infinite goodness, and most amiable perfections, and I purpose by thy holy grace never more to offend thee, and to amend my life. Amen.

## Our Father

Our Father, who art in heaven, hallowed be thy name; thy kingdom come, thy will be done, on earth as it is in heaven. Give us this day our daily bread, and forgive us our trespasses, as we forgive those who trespass against us; and lead us not into temptation, but deliver us from evil. Amen.

## Hail Mary

Hail Mary, full of grace. The Lord is with thee. Blessed art thou amongst women, and blessed is the fruit of thy womb, Jesus. Holy Mary, Mother of God, pray for us sinners, now, and at the hour of our death. Amen.

## Glory be to the Father

Glory be to the Father, and to the Son, and to the Holy Spirit, as it was in the beginning, is now, and ever shall be, world without end. Amen.

## I Believe (The Apostle's Creed)

I believe in God, the Father Almighty, creator of heaven and earth; and in Jesus Christ his only son, Our Lord, who was conceived by the Holy Spirit, born of the

Virgin Mary, suffered under Pontius Pilate, was crucified, died and was buried. He descended into hell; on the third day he rose again from the dead, he ascended into heaven, and is seated at the right hand of God the Father Almighty. From thence he shall come to judge the living and the dead. I believe in the Holy Spirit; the holy Catholic Church; the communion of saints; the forgiveness of sins; the resurrection of the body, and life everlasting. Amen.

THE MEMORARE
Remember, O most loving Virgin Mary, that is a thing unheard of, that anyone ever had recourse to your protection, implored your help, or sought your intercession, and was left forsaken. Filled, therefore, with confidence in your goodness I fly to you, O Mother, Virgin of Virgins. To you I come, before you I stand, a sorrowful sinner. Despite not my poor words, O Mother of the Word of God, but graciously hear and grant my prayer. Amen.

PRAYER TO THE HOLY SPIRIT
Come, O Holy Spirit, fill the hearts of your faithful, and enkindle in them the fire of your love. Send forth your

Spirit and they shall be created and you shall renew the Face of the earth.

*Let us pray*
O God, who through the hearts of the faithful by the light of the Holy Spirit, grant that by the gift of the same Spirit we may be always truly wise and ever rejoice in his consolation through Christ Our Lord. Amen.

PRAYER FOR THE POPE
O almighty and eternal God have mercy on your servant Francis, our Pope, and direct him according to your clemency into the way of everlasting salvation; that he may desire by your grace those things that are agreeable to you, and perform them with all his strength through Christ Our Lord. Amen.

PRAYER FOR THE PRIESTS
Father, you have appointed your son Jesus Christ eternal High Priest. Guide those he has chosen to be ministers of work and sacrament and help them to be faithful in fulfilling the ministry they have received. Grant this through Our Lord Jesus Christ, your son, who lives and reigns with you and the Holy Spirit, one God, forever and ever.

O my God, I most humbly beg of thee to grant me the necessary disposition for assisting devoutly at the adorable sacrifice which I am about to present to thy divine majesty. In union with Jesus Christ, thy beloved son, and with the whole Church, I offer this Mass as a holocaust, to acknowledge thy absolute Dominion over me and all creatures, as sacrifice of thanksgiving for all thy benefits; as a sacrifice of expiation for my sins and the sins of the whole world; and as a sacrifice of impetration to implore for myself and all mankind, the graces and blessings, spiritual and temporal of which we stand most in need. I unite my heart to the dispositions, which animate the Heart of Jesus while he offers himself on the altar, and to those of the Blessed Virgin when she stood at the foot of the Cross. O my divine Jesus grant that, like those who witnessed thy death on Mount Calvary, I may depart from this sanctuary penetrated with compassion for thy sufferings, and with sorrow for my sins by which those sufferings were caused, as likewise with a firm resolution rather to die than ever offend thee more. Amen.

Antiphon. Who is she that cometh forth as the morning rising, fair as the moon, bright as the sun, terrible as an army set in battle array?

My soul doth magnify the Lord.

And my spirit hath rejoiced in God my Saviour.

Because he hath regarded the humility of his handmaid: for behold from henceforth all generations shall call me blessed.

For he that is mighty hath done great things to me, and holy is his name.

And his mercy is from generation unto generations to them that fear him.

He hath showed might in his arm:

He hath scattered the proud in the conceit of their heart.

He hath put down the mighty from their seat: and hath exalted the humble.

He hath filled the hungry with good things: and the rich He hath sent empty away.

He hath received Israel his servant: being mindful of his mercy.

As he spoke to our fathers: to Abraham and to his seed forever.

Glory be to the Father, and to the Son, and to the Holy Spirit.

As it was in the beginning, is now, and ever shall be,

world without end.
Antiphon. Who is she that cometh forth as the morning rising, fair as the
moon, bright as the sun, terrible as an army set in battle array?

V. O Mary, conceived without sin.
R. Pray for us who have recourse to thee.

# *Litany of Praise*

I praise you, Lord Jesus!

You are the King of Kings.

I praise you.

You are the King of Creation.
You are King of the Universe.

I praise you.

You are the Lord of Lords.
You are the Almighty.
You are the Christ.
You are Christ, the King.
You are Lamb of God.

I praise you.

You are the Lion of Judah.
You are the Bright Morning Star.

You are our Champion and Shield.

I praise you.

You are our Strength and our Song.
You are the Way for our life.

I praise you.

You are the Only Truth.
You are the Real Life.
You are the Wonderful Counsellor.
You are the Prince of Peace.

I praise you.

You are the Light of the World.
You are the Living Word.
You are our Redeemer.

I praise you.

You are the Messiah
You are the Anointed One.
You are the Holy One of Israel.
You are the Good Shepherd.

I praise you.

You are the Sheepgate.
You are the Lord of hosts.

I praise you.

You are the Rock of all ages.
You are my Hiding Place.
You are the Saviour of the World
You are the Strong Tower.
You are the Mountain Refuge

I praise you.

You are the Bread of Life
You are the Font of all holiness.
You are the Living Water.
You are the True Vine.
You are my Spouse, my Maker.
You are our Fortress.
You are the Deliverer.
You are our Victory.

I praise you.

You are our Salvation.
You are our Righteousness.

You are our Wisdom.

I praise you.

You are our Sanctification.

I praise you.

You are the Door.
You are the great I Am.

I praise you.

You are the Great High Priest.
You are the Cornerstone.
You are the Sure Foundation.
You are our Joy.
You are our Portion and Cup.

I praise you.

You are my Healing and Wholeness.
You are our Covenant.
You are the Promise of the Father.

I praise you.

You are the Everlasting One.
You are the Lamb that was slain.

I praise you.

You are the Just Judge.
You are the Balm of Gilead.
You are the Mighty Warrior.
You are my Defence.

I praise you.

You are the Bridegroom.
You are my Patience.
You are the Solid Reality.
You are my Provider.
You are the Resurrection and the Life.
You are the Alpha and the Omega.
You are the Beginning and the End.
You are Source, Guide and Goal of all that is.
You are all that I need.

I praise you.

You are all that I want.
You are worthy of all praise!

I praise you.

# *Prayers of Praise taken from Scripture*

PRAYER IN PRAISE OF GODS TIME
Bless the Lord, nights and days,
sing praise to him and highly exalt him forever.
Bless the Lord, light and darkness
sing praise to him and highly exalt him forever.
Bless the Lord, ice and cold,
sing praise to him and highly exalt him forever.
Bless the Lord, frosts and snows,
sing praise to him and highly exalt him forever.
Bless the Lord, lightning and clouds,
sing praise to him and highly exalt him forever.
Let the earth bless the Lord;
let it sing praise to him and highly exalt him forever.
Bless the Lord, mountains and hills,
sing praise to him and highly exalt him forever.


PRAYER IN PRAISE OF GODS PEOPLE
Bless the Lord, you sons of men,
sing praise to him and highly exalt him forever.

Bless the Lord, O Israel,
sing praise to him and highly exalt him forever.
Bless the Lord, you priests of the Lord,
sing praise to him and highly exalt him forever.
Bless the Lord, you servants of the Lord,
sing praise to him and highly exalt him forever.
Bless the Lord, spirits and souls of the righteous,
sing praise to him and highly exalt him forever.
Bless the Lord, you who are holy and humble in heart,
sing praise to him and highly exalt him forever.
Bless the Lord, mountains and hills,
sing praise to him and highly exalt him forever.
Sing praise to him and highly exalt him forever.
For he has rescued us from Hades and saved us from
the hand of death,
and delivered us from the midst of the burning fiery
furnace;
From the midst of the fire he has delivered us.
Give thanks to the Lord, for he is good,
for his mercy endures forever.


PRAYER IN PRAISE OF GODS CREATION
Bless the Lord, you angels of the Lord,
sing praise to him and highly exalt him forever.

Bless the Lord, all waters above the heaven,
sing praise to him and highly exalt him forever.
Bless the Lord, all powers,
sing praise to him and highly exalt him forever.
Bless the Lord, sun and moon,
sing praise to him and highly exalt him forever.
Bless the Lord, stars of heaven,
sing praise to him and highly exalt him forever.
Bless the Lord, all rain and dew,
sing praise to him and highly exalt him forever.
Bless the Lord, all winds,
sing praise to him and highly exalt him forever.
Bless the Lord, fire and heat,
sing praise to him and highly exalt him forever.
Bless the Lord, winter cold and summer heat,
sing praise to him and highly exalt him forever.
Bless the Lord, all dews and snows,
sing praise to him and highly exalt him forever.


PRAYER IN PRAISE OF GODS CREATION
Bless the Lord, all things that grow on the earth,
sing praise to him and highly exalt him forever.
Bless the Lord, you springs,
sing praise to him and highly exalt him forever.

Bless the Lord, seas and rivers,
sing praise to him and highly exalt him forever.
Bless the Lord, you whales and all creatures that move
in waters,
sing praise to him and highly exalt him forever.
Bless the Lord, all birds of the airs,
sing praise to him and highly exalt him forever.
Bless the Lord, all beasts and cattle,
sing praise to him and highly exalt him forever.


PRAYER IN PRAISE OF GODS HOLY NAME
Blessed art thou, O Lord, God of our fathers,
and to be praised and highly exalted forever;
And blessed is thy glorious, holy name
and to be praised and highly exalted forever;
Blessed art thou in the temple of thy holy glory
and to be extolled and highly glorified forever.
Blessed art thou, who sittest upon cherubim and
lookest upon the deeps
and to be praised and highly exalted forever;
Blessed art thou upon the throne of thy kingdom
and to he extolled and highly exalted forever.
Blessed art thou in the firmament of heaven
and to be sung and glorified forever.

Bless the Lord, all works of the Lord,
sing praise to him and highly exalt him forever.
Bless the Lord, you heavens.

For we, O Lord have become fewer than any nation,
and are brought low this day in all the world because
of our sins.
And at this time there is no prince-or-prophet or
healer,
no burnt offerings or sacrifice, or oblation, or incense
no place to make an offering before thee or to find
mercy.
Yet with contrite heart and a humble spirit may we be
accepted,
as though it were with burnt offerings of rams and
bulls,
and with tens of thousands of fat lambs;
such may our sacrifice be in thy sight of this day,
and may we wholly follow thee,
for there will be no shame for those who trust in thee,
And now with all our heart we follow thee,
we fear thee and seek thy face.

Do not put us to shame,
but deal with us in thy forbearance
and in thy abundant mercy.
Deliver us in accordance with marvelous works,
and give glory to thy name O Lord!

# Prayers to the Sacred Heart of Jesus

LITANY OF THE SACRED HEART OF JESUS
Lord, have mercy on us.
Christ, have mercy on us.

Lord, have mercy on us. Christ hear us.
Christ, graciously hear us.

God the Father of heaven,
have mercy on us.

God the Son, Redeemer of the world,
have mercy on us.

God the Holy Spirit,

Holy Trinity, one God.

Heart of Jesus, Son of the Eternal Father,

Heart of Jesus, formed by the Holy Spirit in the womb
of the Virgin Mother.

Heart of Jesus, substantially united with the Word of
God,

Heart of Jesus, of infinite majesty,

Heart of Jesus, holy temple of God,

Heart of Jesus, tabernacle of the Most High,

Heart of Jesus, house of God and gate of heaven,

Heart of Jesus, burning furnace of charity,

Heart of Jesus, abode of justice and love,

Heart of Jesus, full of goodness and love,

Heart of Jesus, full of all virtues,

Heart of Jesus, most worthy of all praise,

Heart of Jesus, king and centre of all hearts,

Heart of Jesus, in whom are all the treasurers of wisdom and knowledge,

Heart of Jesus, in whom dwells the fullness of divinity,

Heart of Jesus, in whom the Father is well pleased,

Heart of Jesus, of whose fullness we have all received,

Heart of Jesus, desire of the everlasting hills,

Heart of Jesus, patient and most merciful,

Heart of Jesus, enriching all who invoke thee,

Heart of Jesus, fountain of life and holiness,

Heart of Jesus, propitiation for our sins,

Heart of Jesus, loaded down with reproaches,

Heart of Jesus, bruised for our offences,

Heart of Jesus, obedient unto death,

Heart of Jesus, pierced with a lance,

Heart of Jesus, source of all consolation,

Heart of Jesus, our life and resurrection,

Heart of Jesus, our peace and reconciliation.

Heart of Jesus, victim for sin,

Heart of Jesus, salvation of those who trust in thee,

Heart of Jesus, hope in those who die in thee,

Heart of Jesus, delight of all the saints,

> Lamb of God, who takest away the sins of the world, spare us, O Lord.
> Lamb of God, who takest away the sins of the world, graciously hear us O Lord.
> Lamb of God, who takest away the sins of the world, have mercy on us.

V. Jesus meek and humble of heart.
R. Make our hearts like unto Thine.

*Let us pray*
O almighty and eternal God, look upon the Heart of thy dearly beloved son, and upon the praise and satisfaction he offers thee on behalf of sinners and for those who

seek thy mercy. Be appeased, we beg of thee and grant us pardon in the name of the same Jesus Christ, thy son, who lives and reigns with thee, world without end. Amen.

THE MORNING PRAYER
O Jesus, through the most pure Heart of Mary, I offer you the prayers, works, joys and sufferings of this day for all the intentions of your divine heart.

ACT OF CONSECRATION OF ONESELF TO THE SACRED HEART
Heart of my Jesus, I consecrate myself and all I love to you. Give us, O sweet and loving Heart, a great love of you, and a zeal for all that concerns you, so that we may labour for your glory and serve you well. O Jesus of the Loving Heart, guard us from evil and cherish us as your own until the time comes to go to you forever. Amen.

CONSECRATION OF HOMES TO THE SACRED HEART
Humbly kneeling at your feet, loving Heart of Our God, we consecrate our home and every home and every one in it and all our interests to you. We beseech you to bless us one and all, and to keep us in your love. Prosper our

undertakings as far as they are for our good and for your glory; comfort us in our afflictions; fill our hearts with your peace, and guard us from every kind of evil. May our lives honour you, and may death find us unafraid. Amen.

A PRAYER TO THE HEART OF JESUS

O most holy Heart of Jesus, fountain of every blessing, I adore you, I love you, and with a lively sorrow for my sins, I offer you this poor heart of mine. Make me humble, patient, pure and wholly obedient to your will. Grant, good Jesus, that I may live in you and for you. Protect me in the midst of danger; comfort me in my afflictions; give me health of body assistance in my temporal needs, your blessing on all that I do, and the grace of a holy death. Sacred Heart of Jesus may your kingdom come.

## Prayers to the Blessed Virgin

THE LITANY OF THE BLESSED VIRGIN
Lord, have mercy.
Lord, have mercy.

Christ, have mercy
Christ, have mercy.

Lord, have mercy
Lord, have mercy.

Christ, hear us.
Christ, graciously hear us.

God the Father of heaven, have mercy on us.

God the Son, Redeemer of the world, have mercy on us.

God the Holy Spirits, have mercy on us.

Holy Trinity, one God, have mercy on us.

| | |
|---|---|
| Holy Mary | Pray for us |
| Holy Mother of God | Pray for us |
| Holy Virgin of Virgins | Pray for us |
| Mother of Christ | Pray for us |

| | |
|---|---|
| Mother of divine grace | Pray for us |
| Mother most pure | Pray for us |
| Mother most chaste | Pray for us |
| Mother inviolate | Pray for us |
| Mother undefiled | Pray for us |
| Mother most lovable | Pray for us |
| Mother most admirable | Pray for us |
| Mother of good counsel | Pray for us |
| Mother of our Creator | Pray for us |
| Mother of our Saviour | Pray for us |
| Virgin most prudent | Pray for us |
| Virgin most venerable | Pray for us |
| Virgin most renowned | Pray for us |
| Virgin most powerful | Pray for us |
| Virgin most merciful | Pray for us |
| Virgin most faithful | Pray for us |
| Mirror of justices | Pray for us |
| Seat of wisdom | Pray for us |
| Cause of our joy | Pray for us |
| Spiritual vessel | Pray for us |
| Singular vessel of devotion | Pray for us |
| Mystical rose | Pray for us |
| Tower of David | Pray for us |

| | |
|---|---|
| Tower of ivory | Pray for us |
| House of gold | Pray for us |
| Ark of the covenant | Pray for us |
| Gate of heaven | Pray for us |
| Morning star | Pray for us |
| Health of the sick | Pray for us |
| Refuge of sinners | Pray for us |
| Comfort of the afflicted | Pray for us |
| Help of Christians | Pray for us |
| Queen of angels | Pray for us |
| Queen of patriarchs | Pray for us |
| Queen of prophets | Pray for us |
| Queen of apostles | Pray for us |
| Queen of martyrs | Pray for us |
| Queen of confessors | Pray for us |
| Queen of virgins | Pray for us |
| Queen of all saints | Pray for us |
| Queen conceived without original sin | Pray for us |
| Queen assumed into heaven | Pray for us |
| Queen of the Most Holy Rosary | Pray for us |
| Queen of Peace | Pray for us |

Lamb of God, you take away the sins of the world, spare us, O Lord.
Lamb of God, you take away the sins of the world, graciously hear us,
O Lord
Lamb of God, you take away the sins of the world, have mercy on us.

Pray for us, O Holy Mother of God.
That we may be made worthy of the promises of Christ.

*Let us pray*
Lord God, give to your people the joy of continual health in mind and body. With the prayers of the Virgin Mary to help us, guide us through the sorrows of this life to eternal happiness in the life to come. Grant this through Our Lord Jesus Christ, your son, who lives and reigns with you and the Holy Spirit, forever and ever. Amen.

THE HOLY ROSARY
The Holy Rosary is composed of fifteen decades, each decade consisting of the 'Our Father', ten 'Hail Marys', and the 'Glory be to the Father', and each being recited in honour of some mystery in the life of Our Lord and

Blessed Mother. During each decade we should call to mind the mystery which it is intended to honour, and pray that we may learn to practice the virtue specially taught us by that mystery.

### I. The Five Joyful Mysteries

1. The Annunciation.
2. The Visitation.
3. The Nativity.
4. The Presentation in the Temple.
5. The Finding of the Child Jesus in the Temple.

### II. The Five Sorrowful Mysteries

1. The Prayer and Agony in the Garden.
2. The Scourging at the Pillar.
3. The Crowning with Thorns.
4. The Carrying of the Cross.
5. The Crucification and Death of Our Lord.

### III. The Five Glorious Mysteries

1. The Resurrection.
2. The Ascension of Christ into heaven.
3. The Descent of the Holy Spirit on the Apostles.
4. The Assumption.
5. The Coronation of the Blessed Virgin Mary in heaven and Glory of all the Saints.

## THE HAIL HOLY QUEEN

Hail, Holy Queen, Mother of mercy; hail, our life, our sweetness, and our hope! To you do we cry, poor banished children of Eve; to you do we send up our sighs, mourning and weeping in this vale of tears. Turn them most gracious advocate, your eyes of mercy towards us; and after this our exile, show us the blessed fruit of your womb, Jesus. O clement, O loving, O sweet Virgin Mary.

V. Pray for us, O Holy Mother of God.
R. That we may be made worthy of the promises of Christ.

*Let us pray*
O God, whose only, begotten son, by his life, death and resurrection, has purchased for us the rewards of eternal life, grant, we beseech you, that meditating on these Mysteries of the Most Holy Rosary of the Blessed Virgin Mary, we may both imitate what they contain, and obtain what they promise, through the same Jesus Christ Our Lord. Amen.

PRAYER TO OUR LADY OF MOUNT CARMEL
O Most Beautiful Flower of Mount Carmel.
Fruitful vine splendour of heaven.
Blessed Mother of the Son of God, pray for us.
O star of the sea help me, show me you are my mother.
O Holy Mary Mother of God, Queen of Heaven
and earth I humbly beseech you from the bottom
of my heart to grant my request.
There are none that can withstand your power.
O show me herein you are my mother.
Sweet Mother I place this cause in your hands.


MEMORARE
Remember, O most Pious Virgin Mary, that it is a thing unheard of that thou ever forsake those who have recourse to thee. Encouraged with this hope and confidence, I cast myself at thy sacred feet humbly deploring my sins and I beseech thee to adopt me for thy Child and take upon thee the care of my eternal salvation. Do not, O Mother of the Word Incarnate, reject my petition but graciously hear it and grant it. Amen. (Prayer Remembered by Andy Proctor)

NOVENA TO OUR LADY OF KNOCK
Give praise to the Father Almighty,
To his son, Jesus Christ the Lord.
To the Spirit who lives in our hearts,
Now and forever. Amen.

Our Lady of Knock, Queen of Ireland, you give hope to
your people in a time of distress, and comfort them in
sorrow. You have inspired countless pilgrims to pray
with confidence to your divine son, remembering his
promise: 'Ask and you shall receive, seek and you shall
find.'
Help me to remember that we are pilgrims on the road
to heaven. Fill me with love and concern for my
brothers and sisters in Christ, especially those who live
with me. Comfort me when I am sick, lonely or
depressed. Teach me how to take part ever more
reverently in the Holy Mass. Give me a greater love for
Jesus in the Blessed Sacrament. Pray for me now, and at
the hour of my death. Amen.

Lamb of God, you take away the sins of the world;
Have mercy on us.
Lamb of God, you take away the sins of the world;
Have mercy on us.
Lamb of God, you take away the sins of the world;
Grant us peace.

SAINT JOSEPH

Chosen by God to be the husband of Mary, the protector of the Holy Family, the guardian of the Church, protect all families in their work and recreation, and guard us on our journey through life.

> Lamb of God, you take away the sins of the world;
> Have mercy on us.
> Lamb of God, you take away the sins of the world;
> Have mercy on us.
> Lamb of God, you take away the sins of the world;
> Grant us peace.

SAINT JOHN

Beloved disciple of the Lord, faithful priest, teacher of the Word of God, help us to hunger for the Word, to be loyal to the Mass, and to love one another and listen to the Gospel and keep the Message deep in our hearts.

> Lamb of God, you take away the sins of the world;
> Have mercy on us.
> Lamb of God, you take away the sins of the world
> Have mercy on us.
> Lamb of God, you take away the sins of the world
> Grant us peace.

| | |
|---|---|
| Our Lady of Knock | Pray for us |
| Refuge of Sinners | Pray for us |
| Queen Assumed into heaven | Pray for us |
| Queen of the Holy Rosary | Pray for us |
| Mother of Nazareth | Pray for us |
| Queen of Virgins | Pray for us |
| Help of Christians | Pray for us |
| Health of the Sick | Pray for us |
| Queen of Peace | Pray for us |
| Our Lady, Queen and Mother | Pray for us |
| Our Lady, Mother of the Church | Pray for us |

*Let us pray*

With the angels and saints let us pray. Give praise to the Father Almighty, to his son, Jesus Christ the Lord, to the Spirit who lives in our hearts, both now and forever. Amen.


THE ANGELUS

V. The Angel of the Lord declared unto Mary.

R And she conceived by the Holy Spirit. Hail Mary ...

V. Behold the handmaid of the Lord.
R. Be it done unto me according to thy word. Hail Mary ...

V. And the Word was made flesh.
R. And dwelt among us. Hail Mary ...

V. Pray for us, O Holy Mother of God.
R. That we may be made worthy of the promises of Christ.

*Let us pray*
Pour forth, we beseech thee, O Lord, thy grace into our hearts that as we have known the incarnation of Christ thy son by the message of an angel, by his Passion and Cross, we may be brought to the glory of his Resurrection through the same Christ Our Lord. Amen.

# *Prayers to the Holy Spirit*

LITANY OF THE HOLY SPIRIT
Lord, have mercy.
Christ, have mercy on us.

Lord, have mercy on us. Christ, hear us.
Christ, graciously hear us.

God, the Father Almighty, have mercy on us.

Jesus, Eternal Son of the Father, Redeemer of the world, save us.

Spirit of the Father and the Son and Infinite Love of Both, sanctify us.

Most Holy Trinity, hear us.

Holy Spirit, who proceeds from the Father and the Son, come to us.

Promise to the Father,
Gift of God Most High,
Ray of heavenly light,
Fount of Living Water,

Consuming Fire,
Author of all good,
Spiritual Union,
Ardent Charity,
Spirit of wisdom,
Spirit of understanding,
Spirit of counsel and of fortitude,
Spirit of knowledge and of piety,
Spirit of the fear of the Lord,
Spirit of truth and of love,
Spirit of grace and of prayer,
Spirit of peace and of sweetness,
Spirit of modesty and of innocence,
Spirit of consolation,
Spirit that governs the Church,
Spirit that fills the universe,
Spirit of adoption of the Son of God,
Holy Spirit, imprint on our hearts a horror for sin,
we beseech you, hear us.
Holy Spirit, come and renew the face of the earth.
Holy Spirit, shed your light upon our understanding.
Holy Spirit, engrave your law upon our hearts.
Holy Spirit, open to us the treasure of your grace.
Holy Spirit, teach us how we ought to pray.
Holy Spirit, enlighten us with your heavenly
inspirations.

Holy Spirit, grant us the knowledge that is necessary.
Holy Spirit, instill into us the practice of the virtues.
Holy Spirit, grant that we may persevere in justice.
Holy Spirit, be our reward.

Lamb of God, who takest away the sins of the world,
send us your Holy Spirit
Lamb of God, who takest away the sins of the world,
imbue us with the spirit of wisdom and the Holy
Spirit
Lamb of God, who takest away the sins of the world,
imbue us with the spirit of wisdom and devotion.

Come, Holy Spirit, fill the hearts of your faithful,
And kindle in them the fire of your love.

*Let us pray*
O God, who instructed the hearts of the faithful by the
light of the Spirit, grant us in the same Spirit to be truly
wise and ever to rejoice in consolation.
Through Christ Our Lord. Amen.

Holy Spirit, spirit of truth, come into our hearts; shed
the brightness of your light upon the nations, so that
they may please you in unity of faith.

Holy Spirit, sweet Guest of my soul, abide in me and grant that I may ever abide in you.

God the Holy Spirit, have mercy on us.

May the grace of the Holy Spirit enlighten our senses and our hearts. May our hearts be cleansed, O Lord, by the inpouring of the Holy Spirit and may he render them fruitful by watering them with his heavenly dew. With all our heart and voice, we acknowledge, we praise, and we bless you God the Father unbegotten; God, the only begotten Son; God, the Holy Spirit, the Paraclete, O holy and undivided Trinity!


PRAYER TO THE HOLY SPIRIT

Holy Spirit, how solemn and full of heavenly blessings was the day on which I was signed with the chrism of salvation in the Sacrament of Confirmation! You then took possession of my soul and made it your temple and dwelling place. You came to help me grow in good and battle against evil. You marked me indelibly as a soldier of Christ.

I thank you, Divine Spirit, for the fullness of graces and gifts which you bestowed on me in your over-flowing love. But when I reflect upon them, I am filled with shame and contrition at my slowness in responding to these graces and my failure to keep a solemn promise to be a faithful and steadfast Christian. I have offended you and even driven you from my heart. Holy Spirit, I am heartily sorry for all the sins I have committed since the day of my Confirmation because they have offended your goodness and love.

I beg you, God, Holy Spirit, remain with me constantly, and inflame my soul with your eternal love. Never let me be separated from you by sin. I ask most humbly that I may be given strength to cooperate with your graces at all times and never neglect the commandments of God, the precepts of the Church, or the duties of my calling. Let me rather die than ever grieve you by mortal sin.

Come, Holy Spirit, fill the hearts of your faithful and enkindle in them the fire of your love.

Send forth your Spirit, and they shall be created; and you shall renew the face of the earth.

*Let us pray*
O God, who instructed the hearts of the faithful by the light of the Holy Spirit, grant us in the same Spirit to be truly wise and ever to rejoice in his consolation through Christ Our Lord. Amen.

PRAYER TO THE HOLY SPIRIT

Come, O Holy Spirit, fill the hearts of your faithful,
and enkindle in them the fire of your love.
Send forth your Spirit and they shall be created.
And you shall renew the face of the earth.

*Let us pray*
O God, who taught the hearts of the faithful by the light
of the Holy Spirit grant that by the gift of the same Spirit
we may be always truly wise and ever rejoice in his
consolation. Through Christ Our Lord. Amen.

# Prayers to St Joseph

SHORT DAILY ACT OF CONSECRATION TO ST JOSEPH
Blessed Joseph, faithful guardian of my Redeemer Jesus Christ, protector of your chaste spouse the Immaculate Virgin, Mary, Mother of God, I choose you this day to be my special patron and advocate, and I firmly resolve to honour you as such from now and forever. Therefore, I humbly beseech you to receive me for your client, to instruct me in every doubt, to comfort me in every affliction, and finally, to defend and protect me in the hour of my death. Amen.

THE LITANY OF ST JOSEPH
(Recited slowly and meditatively, this becomes a comforting and powerful prayer)
Lord, have mercy on us.
Christ, have mercy on us.
Lord, have mercy.
Christ, hear us.
Christ, graciously hear us.

God the Father of Heaven.
God the Son, Redeemer of the world.
God the Holy Spirit,
Holy Trinity, one God.

Holy Mary,
St Joseph,
Illustrious, descendant of David,
Light of Patriarchs,
Spouse of the Mother of God,
Chaste-guardian of the Virgin,
Foster-father of the Son of God,
Watchful defender of Christ,
Head of the Holy Family,
Joseph most just,
Joseph most pure,
Joseph most prudent,
Joseph most courageous,
Joseph most obedient,
Joseph most faithful,
Mirror of patience,
Lover of Poverty,
Model of all who labour,
Glory of family life,
Guardian of virgins,
Mainstay of families,

Solace of the afflicted,
Hope of the sick,
Patron of the dying,
Terror of demons,
Protector of Holy Church.

Lamb of God, who takes away the sins of the world,
spare us, O Lord
Lamb of God, who takes away the sins of the world,
graciously hear us, O Lord.
Lamb of God, who takes away the sins of the world,
have mercy on us, O Lord.

NOVENA PRAYER TO ST JOSEPH
Ever glorious Joseph, good and faithful servant, God the
Father committed his own family to your care; he
appointed you guardian of his son conceived by the
Holy Spirit in the chaste womb of your virgin spouse,
chose you to be the loving husband and companion of
Mary, mother of Jesus; and he thus called you to play
an important role in his great plan for the redemption
of the human race.

You, blessed Joseph, were privileged to live daily in
the presence of Jesus and of Mary and to die in their
arms. Chase husband of the Mother of God, model and

patron of all who lead pure lives, ever humble, patient and reserved, accept these novena prayers of ours in testimony of our sincere devotion and obtain for us, through your powerful intercession, the particular graces and favours we ask for in this Novena.

MEMORARE TO ST JOSEPH
Remember, most pure spouse of Mary, ever virgin, my loving protector, St Joseph, that never has it been heard that anyone ever invoked your protection, or sought your aid, without being consoled. In this confidence I come before you. I fervently recommend myself to you. Despise not my prayer, virgin father of the Redeemer, but in your pity receive it. Amen.

PRAYER TO ST JOSEPH FOR PURITY OF MIND AND HEART
Guardian of virgins, and holy father, Joseph, to whose faithful custody Christ Jesus, innocence itself, and Mary, Virgin of Virgins, were committed, I pray and beseech you by these dear pledges – Jesus and Mary – that, being preserved from all uncleanness, I may with spotless mind, pure heart, and chaste body, ever serve Jesus and Mary most chastely all the days of my life. Amen.

Ever blessed and glorious Joseph, kind and indulgent father, and compassionate friend of all in sorrow, through that bitter grief with which your heart was saturated when you beheld the sufferings of the infant Saviour and when the prophetic view you contemplated his most ignominious Passion and death, take pity, I beseech you, on my poverty and needs, counsel me in my doubts, and console me in all anxieties.

You are the good father and protector of orphans, the advocate of the defenceless, the patron of those who are in need and desolate. Do not, then, disregard the petition of your poor child.

Listen, then with a father's solicitude to my earnest prayer and obtain for me the object of my special petition. I ask it by the infinite mercy of the eternal Son of God, which induced him to assume our nature, and to be born into this world of sorrow.

AN ACT OF CONSECRATION TO ST JOSEPH

Glorious Patriarch and Patron of the Catholic Church – O virgin spouse of the virgin Mother of God, and guardian and foster-father of the Incarnate Word, in the presence of Jesus and Mary, I choose you this day to be my guardian and my father. God has constituted you head of the Holy Family; accept me, I beseech you, though utterly unworthy; to be a poor little servant in your holy house. Present me to your immaculate spouse; ask her to accept me as a servant and to adopt me as a child. You are a master of the interior life, teach me how to converse constantly with Jesus, and how to serve him faithfully in all things to the end of my life.

# The Passion, Death and Resurrection of Jesus

THE LITANY OF THE PASSION
Lord, have mercy.
Christ, have mercy.
Lord, have mercy on us.
Christ, hear us.
Christ, graciously hear us.
God the Father of heaven, have mercy on us.

God the Son, Redeemer of the world,
Have mercy on us.
God the Holy Spirit,
Have mercy on us.
Holy Trinity, one God,
Have mercy on us.
Jesus, the eternal Wisdom,
Have mercy on us.
Jesus, sold for thirty pieces of silver,
Have mercy on us.

Jesus, in your Agony, bathed in a blood sweat,
Have mercy on us.
Jesus, betrayed by Judas with a kiss,
Have mercy on us.
Jesus, forsaken by your disciples,
Have mercy on us.
Jesus, brought before Annas and Caiphas,
Have mercy on us.
Jesus, accused by false witnesses,
Have mercy on us.
Jesus, spit upon in the face,
Have mercy on us.
Jesus, blindfolded,
Have mercy on us.
Jesus, bitten on the cheek,
Have mercy on us.
Jesus, three times denied by Peter,
Have mercy on us.
Jesus, despised and mocked by Herod,
Have mercy on us.
Jesus, rejected for Barabbas,
Have mercy on us.
Jesus, torn with scrouges,
Have mercy on us.
Jesus, despised as a leper,
Have mercy on us.

Jesus, crowned with thorns,
Have mercy on us.
Jesus, condemned to a shameful death,
Have mercy on us.
Jesus loaded with the heavy weight of the Cross,
Have mercy on us.
Jesus, fastened with nails to the Cross,
Have mercy on us.
Jesus, praying to your Father for your murderers,
Have mercy on us.
Jesus, reviled by the unrepentant thief,
Have mercy on us.
Jesus, promising paradise to the penitent thief,
Have mercy on us.
Jesus, entrusting John to your mother as her son,
Have mercy on us.
Jesus, declaring yourself forsaken by your Father,
Have mercy on us.
Jesus, in your thirst given gall and vinegar to drink,
Have mercy on us.
Jesus, declaring that all things that were written you
fulfilled,
Have mercy on us.
Jesus, commending your Spirit into the hands of your
Father,
Have mercy on us.

Jesus, obedient even to death of the Cross,
Have mercy on us.
Jesus, pierced with a lance,
Have mercy on us.
Jesus, made a victim for us,
Have mercy on us.

So that you may spare us,
we beseech you to hear us.
So that you may pardon us,
we beseech you to hear us.
So that you may bring us to true repentance,
we beseech you to hear us.
So that you may mercifully pour into our hearts the
grace of the Holy Spirit,
we beseech you to hear us.
So that you may unite us to the company of your
saints,
we beseech you to hear us.

Lamb of God, who takest away the sins of the world;
Spare us, O Lord.
Lamb of God, who takest away the sins of the world;
graciously hear us, O Lord.
Lamb of God, who takest away the sins of the world,
have mercy on us.

Christ, hear us.
Christ, graciously hear us.
Lord, have mercy on us.
Christ, have mercy on us.
Lord, have mercy on us.

V. We adore thee, O Christ, and we bless thee.
R. Because by thy holy Cross thou has redeemed the world.

THE PASSION, DEATH AND RESURRECTION OF JESUS
Jesus suffered and died for each one of us. But his Father raised him in glory. We suffer. Let us suffer with faith, with hope and with love. Let us suffer with patience knowing that God's plan for us is infinitely wise and infinitely lovable.

* * *

O Blessed Trinity have mercy on us.
O Heavenly Father, you have created me for perfect happiness. In all humility, I pray, lead me to it, as you please, down the steep cliffs and sufferings in my daily life. Everywhere I will follow you; only show me the way. O Jesus, you have sacrificed everything for my

salvation. And for me you have chosen the same road of suffering. Strengthen me for the suffering. O Holy Spirit, enlighten me in the hours of darkness and temptation, that I may neither go astray nor live in deadly error. Amen.

* * *

Christ, our king, you have descended from the throne of the Cross to reign in tender hearts. From the throne of the Cross, you have shown humankind the road to the land of happiness. On the throne of the Cross you have opened to us the marvelous riches of your heart. Lead us your Way at all times. For this we thank you. Amen.

* * *

A hard day of toil is dawning. O Blessed Trinity, I wish to glorify you by patience and respect for all I meet. Give me wisdom and strength to endure calmly all misunderstanding, contempt and hatred. Unite us all by lively faith, unquenchable hope and love that knows no bounds. Amen.

THE PASSION AND DEATH OF JESUS

The chief priests plotted against Jesus.

Judas agrees to betray Jesus.

Jesus suffers the Agony in the garden of Gethsemane.

Jesus is arrested.

Jesus is taken before the Council. The Council voted against him. He is guilty of death. Some spat on him. They blindfold him and Peter denies that he knew Jesus. The Council put Jesus in chains and sent him to Pilate. Barabbas, a murderer, is preferred to Jesus and set free. Jesus is sentenced to death. Then he is whipped.

Jesus is mocked by the soldiers. A crown of thorny branches is put on his head. They spat on him and hit him over the head with a stick.

Then the soldiers led out Jesus in Calvary to be crucified.

Jesus was crucified at Calvary and his Cross was between two criminals.

Jesus cried out, 'Father into your hands I place my spirit.' He said this and died.


THE RESURRECTION OF JESUS

Two men in bright shining clothes told the women, 'He is not here.' He has been raised. The two disciples conversed with Jesus on the road to Emmaus. Their eyes were opened and they recognised him.

Jesus appeared to his disciples. He gave them the power to forgive sins.

Jesus appeared to Thomas and showed him his wounds.

Lord, by your Cross and Resurrection, you have set me free. You are my Saviour. Amen.

THE DIVINE PRAISES

Blessed be God.

Blessed be his holy name.

Blessed be Jesus Christ, true God and true Man.

Blessed be the name of Jesus.

Blessed be his most Sacred Heart.

Blessed be his most Precious Blood.

Blessed be Jesus in the most holy Sacrament of the Altar.

Blessed be the Holy Spirit, the Paraclete.

Blessed be the great Mother of God, Mary most holy.

Blessed be her holy and Immaculate Conception.

Blessed be her glorious Assumption.

Blessed be the name of Mary, virgin and mother.

Blessed be St Joseph, her spouse most chaste.

Blessed be God in his angels and in his saints.

# The Stations of the Cross

*I. Jesus is condemned to death*
Consider how Jesus, after having been scourged and crowned with thorns, was unjustly condemned by Pilate to die on the Cross.

*II. Jesus receives the Cross*
Consider how Jesus, in making this journey with the Cross on his shoulders, thought of us, and offered for us to his Father the death he was about to undergo.

*III. Jesus falls the first time under his Cross*
Consider the first fall of Jesus under his Cross, his flesh was torn by the scourges, his head was crowned with thorns; he had lost a great quantity of blood. So weakened he could scarcely walk, he yet had to carry this great load upon his shoulders. The soldiers struck him readily and he fell several times.

*IV. Jesus is met by his Blessed Mother*
Consider this meeting of the Son and the Mother, which took place on this journey. Their looks became like arrows to wound those hearts which loved each other so tenderly.

*V. The Cross is laid upon Simon of Cyrene*
Consider how his cruel tormentors, seeing that Jesus was on the point of expiring, and fearing he would die on the way, whereas they wished him to die the shameful death of the Cross, constrained Simon of Cyrene to carry the Cross behind Our Lord.

*VI. Veronica wipes the face of Jesus*
Consider how the holy woman named Veronica seeing Jesus so ill-used, and bathed in sweat and blood, wiped his face with a towel, on which was left the impression of his holy countenance.

*VII. Jesus falls the second time*
Consider the second fall of Jesus under the Cross; a fall which renews the pain of all the wounds in his head and members.

*VIII. The women of Jerusalem mourn for Our Lord*
Consider how these women wept with compassion at seeing Jesus in such a pitiable state, streaming with blood, as he walked along. 'Daughters of Jerusalem,' said he, 'weep not for me, but for yourselves and for your children.'

*IX. Jesus falls for the third time*
Consider the third fall of Jesus Christ. His weakness was extreme, and the cruelty of his executioners was excessive, who tried to hasten his steps when he could scarcely move.

*X. Jesus is stripped of his garments*
Consider the violence with which Jesus was stripped by the executioners. His inner garments adhered to his torn flesh, and they dragged them off so roughly that the skin came with them. Take pity on your Saviour thus cruelly treated.

*XI. Jesus is nailed to the Cross*
Consider how Jesus, having been placed upon the Cross, extended his hands, and offered to his Eternal Father the sacrifice of his life for our salvation. Those

barbarians fastened him with nails, and then, securing the Cross, allowed him to die with anguish on this infamous gibbet.

## XII. *Jesus dies on the Cross*
Consider how Jesus, being consumed with anguish after three hours of agony on the Cross, abandoned himself to the weight of his body, bowed his head and died.

## XIII. *Jesus is taken down from the Cross*
Consider how after Our Lord had expired, two of his disciples Joseph and Nicodemus, took him down from the Cross and placed him in the arms of his afflicted mother, who received him with unutterable tenderness, and pressed him to her bosom.

## XIV. *Jesus is placed in the sepulchre*
Consider how the disciples, accompanied by his holy mother, carried the body of Jesus to bury it. They closed the tomb, and all came sorrowfully away.

# Chaplet of Divine Mercy

THE OUR FATHER
Our Father, who art in heaven,
hallowed be thy name;
thy kingdom come,
thy will be done,
on earth as it is in heaven.
Give us this day our daily bread,
and forgive us our trespasses,
as we forgive those who trespass against us;
and lead us not into temptation,
but deliver us from evil. Amen.


THE HAIL MARY
Hail Mary, full of grace.
The Lord is with thee.
Blessed are thou amongst women,
and blessed is the fruit of your womb, Jesus.
Holy Mary, Mother of God,

pray for us sinners,
now and at the hour of our death. Amen.


THE APOSTLES' CREED
I believe in God, the Father Almighty,
Creator of heaven and earth.
I believe in Jesus Christ, his only son, Our Lord.
He was conceived by the power of the Holy Spirit,
Born of the Virgin Mary,
He suffered under Pontius Pilate,
Was crucified, died and was buried.
He descended to the dead.
On the third day he rose again.
He ascended into heaven,
and is seated at the right hand of the Father.
He will come again to judge the living and the dead.
I believe in the Holy Spirit,
the holy Catholic Church,
the communion of saints,
the forgiveness of sins,
the resurrection of the body,
and life everlasting. Amen.

Eternal Father,
I offer you the Body and Blood,
Soul and Divinity
of your dearly beloved son,

Our Lord Jesus Christ,
in atonement for our sins
and those of the whole world. (repeat once)

For the sake of his sorrowful Passion
have mercy on us and on the whole world. (repeat ten times)

Holy God, Holy Mighty One,
Holy Immortal One,
have mercy on us and on the whole world. (repeat three times)

# Prayers to the Holy Angels

LITANY TO THE HOLY ANGELS

| | |
|---|---|
| Holy Mary, Queen of Angles | Pray for me |
| St Michael | Pray for me |
| St Michael, filled with the wisdom of God | Pray for me |
| St Michael, perfect adorer of the Incarnate Word | Pray for me |
| St Michael, crowned with honor and glory | Pray for me |
| St Michael, most powerful prince of the armies of the Lord | Pray for me |
| St Michael, standard-bearer of the most Holy Trinity | Pray for me |
| St Michael, guardian of paradise | Pray for me |
| St Michael, guide and comforter of the people of Israel | Pray for me |
| St Michael, splendor and fortress of the Church Militant | Pray for me |

| | |
|---|---|
| St Michael, honour and joy of the Church Triumphant | Pray for me |
| St Michael, light of angels | Pray for me |
| St Michael, bulwark of orthodox believers | Pray for me |
| St Michael, strength of those who fight under the standard of the Cross | Pray for me |
| St Michael, light and confidence of souls at the hour of death, | Pray for me |
| St Michael, our most sure aid | Pray for me |
| St Michael, our help in all adversities | Pray for me |
| St Michael, herald of the everlasting sentence | Pray for me |
| St Michael, consoler of souls detained in the flames of purgatory | Pray for me |
| St Michael, whom the Lord has charged to receive souls after death | Pray for me |
| St Michael, our prince | Pray for me |
| St Michael, our advocate | Pray for me |

Pray for us, O glorious St Michael, Prince of the Church of Jesus Christ, That we may be worthy of the promises of Christ. O most Holy Trinity, who are dwelling by your grace within my soul, I adore you. O most Holy Trinity, who are dwelling by your grace within my soul, make me love you more and more. O most Holy Trinity, who are dwelling by your grace within my soul, sanctify me more and more. Abide with me, O Lord and be my true joy.

### PRAYER TO MY GUARDIAN ANGEL

My dear Guardian Angel, you were given to me by my merciful God to be the faithful companion of my earthly exile. I honour and love you as my most devoted friend to whom God has entrusted the care of my immortal soul. With all my heart I thank you for your love and constant care of me.

Dearest angel-friend, I beg you to guard and protect me, a poor sinner. Conduct me on the way of life. Warn me against every occasion of sin, and fill my soul with wholesome thoughts and loving encouragement to practise virtue. Intercede for me that I may share in your burning zeal in God's service and devoted love for his divine Will.

Forgive me, loving Guardian, for so often disregarding your advice in the past and for ignoring your aspirations. I promise in the future to obey you willingly and faithfully. You know the value of my soul in the eyes of God. Never permit me to forget that it was redeemed by the Precious Blood of Jesus Christ. Let no stain of evil disfigure the beauty of my soul, nor any sinful thought or deed rob me of my dignity as a child of God. Keep me from scandal that I may never become an occasion of sin to others and thus destroy the work which Christ has wrought in their souls by his bitter Passion and death.

Dear Guardian Angel, I thank God who has daily shown his mercy to me through you. May I show my gratitude by following your guidance. May I enjoy your protection in this dangerous journey through life that I may reach my eternal home in heaven, there to praise the mercy of God towards me in union with you and all the other angels and saints forever. Amen.

Angel of God, my guardian dear,
To whom his love commits me here,
Ever this day be at my side,
To light and guard, to rule and guide. Amen.

BEHOLD MY GUARDIAN ANGEL

My dear Guardian Angel, I beg you to plead with God for me that I may always keep my life pure and happy. Protect me from the many dangers that confront me on my journey through life. Strengthen me in my struggle against the temptations of the world, the flesh, and the devil.

My loving angel-friend, help me to be pure in thought, desire, word, deed in imitation of Jesus, the Lover of Pure Souls, and of Mary, the Virgin of Virgins. Obtain for me a deep sense of modesty, which will be reflected in my external conduct.

I beg you, gentle angel, to be the guardian of my purity. For your great love for Jesus, the King of Angels and for Mary, the Queen of the Angels, keep me from all uncleanness, and grant that my mind may be unstained, my heart pure, and my body chaste. Help me always to serve Jesus and long to those of whom Jesus spoke: 'Blessed are the pure of heart, for they shall see God.' Amen.


PRAYER TO SAINT MICHAEL

Saint Michael the Archangel, defend us in battle, be our protection against the wickedness and snares of the devil. May God rebuke him, we humbly pray; and may you, O Prince of the Heavenly Host, by the power of God thrust into hell Satan and all evil spirits who wander through the world for the ruin of souls.

St Michael the Archangel, defend us in the battle, that we may not perish in the fearful judgment. Saint Michael, first champion of the kingship of Christ, pray for us. Amen.

PRAYER TO SAINT GABRIEL

O God, since you choose the Archangel Gabriel from among all the angels to announce the mystery of your incarnation, mercifully grant that we who solemnly keep his feast on earth may feel the benefit of his patronage in heaven. Who lives and reigns forever. Amen.

PRAYER TO SAINT RAPHAEL

Holy Archangel Raphael, standing close to the throne of God and offering him our prayers, I venerate you as God's special friend and messenger. God has singled you out to be the Angel of Youth, for he entrusted the young Tobias to your care. I choose you as my patron and wish to love and obey you as Tobias did. I consecrate to you my body and soul, and all my work, and my whole life. I want you to be my guide and counselor in all the dangerous and difficult problems and decisions of my life. Remember, dearest Saint Raphael, that the grace of God preserved you with the good angels in heaven when the proud ones were cast into hell. I entreat you, therefore, to help me in my struggle against the world, the flesh and the devil. Defend me from all dangers and every occasion of sin. Direct me always in the way of peace, safety, and salvation. Offer my prayers to God as you offered those of Tobias so that, through your intercession, I may obtain the graces necessary for the salvation of my soul. Help me to love and serve God faithfully, to die in his grace, and finally to merit to join you in seeing and praising God forever in heaven. Amen. O Lord God, be pleased to send our aid Saint Raphael the Archangel. May he who always stands before the throne of your Majesty, offer to you in our humble petitions for your blessing. Through Christ Our Lord. Amen.

TEACHING OF THE ANGELS

In the beginning of time God created spiritual essences (angels) out of nothing.

The nature of the angels is spiritual.

The angels are by nature immortal.

God set a supernatural final end for the angels, the immediate vision of God and endowed them with sanctifying grace in order that they might achieve this end.

The angels were subjected to a moral testing.

The evil spirits (demons) were created good by God' they became evil through their own fault.

The primary task of the good angels is the glorification and the service of God.

The secondary task of the good angels is the protection of men and care for their salvation.

Every one of the faithful has his own special guardian angel from Baptism.

The Devil possesses a certain dominion over mankind by reason of Adam's sin.

Angels have been present since creation and throughout the history of salvation, announcing this salvation from afar or near and serving the accomplishment of the divine plan: they closed the earthly paradise; protected Lot; saved Hagar and her child; stayed Abraham's hand; communicated the law by their ministry; led the People of God; announced births and callings; and assisted the prophets, just to cite a few examples. Finally the angel Gabriel announced the birth of the Saviour Jesus himself.

# Prayers for Peace

PRAYER FOR PEACE

Loving Father, your will is that we should all be of one mind in our land. God of peace, bless Ireland and bless those countries where there is civil strife, where neighbour rises up against neighbourhood, where familiar streets become battle fields, and familiar people the casualties. Change the hearts of all who think that their cause is more important than a persons life. Change the politics of those on either side which create, condone or extend conflict. And by the power of the Cross help all who sin to repent, and all who have been sinned against to forgive so that peace may come through Christ Our Lord.

(Prayer by the late Albert Reynolds, former Taoiseach of Ireland)

PRAYER FOR PEACE OF POPE BENEDICT XV
(As ordered to be publicly recited in all Catholic
Churches in Ireland by the Irish Hierarchy 24 June
1940)

Dismayed by the horrors of a war which is bringing ruin
to peoples and nations, we turn O Jesus, to thy most
loving heart with tears we invoke thee to end this
fearful scourge; O King of Peace, we humbly implore
the peace for which we long. From thy Sacred Heart
thou didst shed forth over the world divine charity, so
that discord might end and love alone might reign
among men. During thy life on earth thy heart bled with
tender compassion for the sorrows of men; in this hour
made terrible with burning hate, with bloodshed and
with slaughter, once more may thy divine heart be
moved to pity. Pity the countless mothers in anguish for
the fate of their sons; pity the numberless families now
bereaved of their fathers; pity Europe, over which
broods such havoc and disaster. Do thou inspire rulers
and peoples with counsels of meekness, do thou heal
the discords that tear the nations asunder; thou Who
didst shed thy Precious Blood that they might love as
brothers, bring men together once more in loving
harmony. And as once before, to the cry of the Apostle
Peter; Save us, Lord we perish, thou didst still the raging
waves, so now design to hear our trustful prayer, and

give back to the world peace and tranquility. And do thou, O Most Holy Virgin, as in other times of sore distress, be thou our help, our protection and our safeguard. Amen.

PRAYER FOR UNITY IN CHRIST

Lord Jesus, who on the eve of your death, prayed that all your disciples might be one, as you in the Father and the Father in you, make us feel intense sorrow over the infidelity of our disunity. Give us the honesty to recognise, and the courage to reject, whatever indifferences towards one another, or mutual distrust, or even which lie hidden within us. Enable all of us to meet one another in you. And let your prayer for the unity of Christians, be ever in our hearts and on our lips, unity such as you desire it and by the means that you will make us find the way that leads to unity in you who are perfect charity, through being obedient to the spirit of love and truth. Amen.

# Healing Prayers

PRAYER FOR THE SOULS IN PURGATORY

Eternal Father, I offer you the most Precious Blood of your divine son. Jesus, in union with the Masses, said throughout the world today, for all the holy souls in Purgatory, for sinners everywhere, for sinners in the universal church, those in my own home and within my own family.

THE MIRACLE PRAYER

Lord Jesus, I come before you, just as I am. I am sorry for my sins, I repent of my sins. Please forgive me. In your name, I forgive all others for what they have done against me. I renounce Satan, the evil spirits and all their works. I give you my entire self. Lord Jesus, now and forever, I invite you into my life Jesus. I accept you as my Lord, God and Saviour. Heal me, change me, strengthen me in body, soul and spirit.

Come Lord Jesus, cover me with your Precious Blood, and fill me with your Holy Spirit. I love you Lord

Jesus. I praise you, Lord Jesus. I thank you, Jesus. I shall follow you every day of my life. Amen.

Mary, my mother, Queen of Peace,
all the Angels and Saints, please help me. Amen.
(By Fr Peter Rookey)


PRAYER FOR HEALING
When we pray this prayer, Our Lord gently and gradually removes layers of emotional scar tissue while we sleep, allowing us to be happier people.


PRAYER AT BEDTIME
Jesus, through the power of the Holy Spirit, go back into my memory as I sleep. Every hurt that has ever been done to me … heal that hurt. Every hurt that I have ever caused to another person … heal that hurt. All the relationships that have been damaged in my whole life that I am not aware off … heal those relationships. But Lord, if there is anything that I need to do…if I need to go to a person because he is still suffering from my hand, bring to my awareness that person. I choose to forgive, and I ask to be forgiven. Remove whatever

bitterness may be in my heart, Lord and fill the empty spaces with your Love. Thank you Jesus. Amen.
(By Fr Peter Rookey)


PRAYER OF DELIVERANCE BASED ON SCRIPTURE

Lord Jesus Christ, I believe that you are the Son of God and the only way to God; and that you died on the Cross for my sins and rose again from the dead. 'I give up all my sins before you and ask for your forgiveness especially for any sins that exposed me to a curse. Release me also from the consequences of my ancestors sins. By a decision of my will, I forgive all who have harmed me or wronged me – just as I want God to forgive me. In particular I forgive …

I renounce all contact with anything occult or satanic – if I have any 'contact objects', I commit myself to destroy them. I cancel all Satan's claims against me. Lord Jesus, I believe that on the Cross you took on yourself every curse that could ever come upon me. So I ask you now to release me from every curse in my life – in your name, Lord Jesus Christ.

My body is a temple for the Holy Spirit, redeemed, cleansed and sanctified by the blood of Jesus. My members – the parts of my body – are instruments of righteousness, presented to God for his service and for his glory. The devil has no place in me, no power over me, no unsettled claims against me. All has been settled by the blood of Jesus. I overcome Satan by the blood of the Lamb and by the word of my testimony, and I do not love my life to death. My body is for the Lord, and the Lord is for my body. (Based on 1 Corinthians 6:19; Ephesians 1:7; John 1:7, Hebrews 13:12; Romans 6:13; 8:33–4; Revelation 12:11; 1 Corinthians 6:13)

THE HEALING PRAYER

Lord Jesus I come before you, just as I am. I am sorry for my sins. I repent of my sins, please forgive me. In your name I forgive all others for what they have done against me. I renounce Satan, the evil spirits and all their works.

I give you my entire self. Lord Jesus, now and forever, I invite you into my life, Jesus. I accept you as my Lord, God and Saviour. Heal me, change me, strengthen me in body, soul and spirit.

Come Lord Jesus, cover me with your Precious Blood, and fill me with your Holy Spirit. I thank you, Jesus. I shall follow you every day of my life. Amen.

Mary, my mother, Queen of Peace, all the Angels and Saints please help me. Amen.

PRAYER FOR UNITY IN CHRIST

Lord Jesus,

who on the eve of your death,

prayed that all your disciples might be one,

as you in the Father and the Father in you,

make us feel intense sorrow over the infidelity of our disunity.

Give us the honesty to recognise,

and the courage to reject,

whatever indifference towards one another,

or mutual distrust, or even enmity lie hidden within us.

Enable all of us to meet one another in you.

And let your prayer for the unity of Christians,

be ever in our hearts and on our lips –

unity such as you desire it and by the means that you will.

Make us find the way that leads to unity in you who are perfect charity, through being obedient to the spirit of love and truth. Amen.

# Prayers to the Irish Saints

THE LITANY OF THE IRISH SAINTS

| | |
|---|---|
| St Patrick | Grant us Faith |
| St Brigid | |
| St Colmcille | |
| St Kevin | Teach us |
| St Brendan | |
| St Kieran | |
| St Carthagh | Pray for us |
| St Colman | |
| St Kilian | |
| St Declan | Heal us |
| St Fiacre | |
| St Canice | Grant us Wisdom |
| St Gall | |
| St Otteran | |
| St Malachy | Grant us Understanding |

| | |
|---|---|
| St Laurence O'Toole | |
| St Columba | Grant us Knowledge |
| St Fergal | |
| St Finnian | Grant us Piety |
| St Mollining | |
| St Attracta | |
| St Aidan | Grant us Love |
| St Oliver Plunkett | |
| St Mel | |
| St Mainchin | Grant us Forgiveness |
| St Laserian | |
| St Finlough | Grant us the Spirit of God |
| St Conleth | |
| The Irish Martyrs | |
| All The Irish Saints | Intercede for our Country |

PRAYERS TO ST PATRICK

O great Apostle of Ireland, glorious St Patrick, to whom under God, so many are indebted for the most precious of all treasures, the great gift of Faith, receive labours, the precious light of faith, and beg for us the glorious rays that have long since beamed, the grace to regulate our lives by its sacred maxims.

* * *

God Our Father, you sent St Patrick to preach your glory
to the people of Ireland. By the help of his prayers may
all Christians proclaim your love to all men. Through
Jesus Christ Our Lord. Amen.

* * *

Lord Our God, may all we do and say proclaim your
truth in imitation of St Patrick who did not spare
himself but gave his whole life through the preaching
of your Word. Grant this through Jesus Christ Our Lord.
Amen.

St Patrick's Breast Plate
I arise today
in power and might.
I call upon the Trinity,
with faith in the threeness,
and trust in the oneness
of the great world's Maker.
I arise today
in the power and might
of Christ's birth and baptism,

His crucifixion and burial,
His Resurrection, his ascension,
His coming anew to judge mankind.

Christ save me today
from poison and from burning,
from drowning, from wounding,
from grace abounding
may be my reward.

Christ be with me,
Christ within me,
Christ before me,
Christ behind me,
Christ beneath and Christ above,
Christ on my right hand,
Christ on my left.
Christ with me walking,
waking and sleeping.
Christ in every heart thinking of me,
Christ in every eye that sees me.
Christ in every ear that hears me.

PRAYER TO ST PATRICK

St Patrick, patron saint of our Isle, chosen by God to bring the faith to Ireland, come walk among us again and intercede for us to the most kind Father, through his only begotten son for an outpouring of the Holy Spirit upon our nation. Inspire the leaders of our country and elected representatives to enact just laws which will be in accordance with the holy will of God. Protect and guide our bishops and priests and keep them safe in God's love and service. Guide your flock on the right path, dissolve the hatreds, the injustices in our country, melt all hearts and make them one. Grant that Christian families may desire to be distinguished by giving to your church of tomorrow saintly priests, heroic missionaries, gentle and tireless sisters.

HAIL GLORIOUS ST PATRICK

Hail, glorious St Patrick! We honour thy name,
Tho' Erin may claim thee, the world knows thy fame.
The faith of our fathers is our treasure too,
How holy the thought, that they learned it from you
Thru crosses and trails its fires burn bright,
They show us the way, and the truth, and the light,
Great Saint! Intercede, that we always may be
Devoted and loyal, true children of thee.

Our love and devotion be ever like thine,
Our thought be of Jesus, our heart be his shrine.
And when to the end of life's path we have trod,
Be near us great Bishop, anointed of God.

*St Patrick*
St Patrick, Apostle of the Gael, keep the light of the True
Faith, ever brightly burning in the hearts of our people!
St Brigid, Mary of the Gael, keep the virtues of chastity
and humility in our hearts and homes forever!


*A Prayer to St Patrick*
Fifteen centuries of faithful striving
To walk, O Patrick in the ways you trod–
The Fifteen Mysteries of Ireland's Rosary,
Told unceasingly for love of God!
Sometimes joyful and sometimes glorious
Ah! how often sorrowful, with pain and tears.
O Patrick! Beg from Our Lord for Ireland,
The reward of those fifteen hundred years.

*Old Irish Prayer to Saint Colmcille*
O Colmcille, friendly and gentle; in the
name of the Father, the Son and the Holy
Ghost, by the Trinity, by the Three,
aid us and guard our path. Amen.


*Prayer for an Exile*
St Colmcille, who suffered pain and grief of exile, watch
over the children of Ireland, scattered throughout the
world. Obtain for them solace and courage, and keep
them true to God in every trial and temptation!


PRAYERS FOR ST BRIGID


*Mary of Ireland*
From all sin and harm, from all danger and woe, guard
me, Mary of Ireland, wherever I go. O Brigid, be with
me until the road's end; O help me to pass through that
Gare of God's friend.


*Heart of Generosity*
Brigid, Mary of our race. Win for us God's sheltering
grace. Heart of generosity, keep us from all evil free.

Heart of love and holiness, ask God our every act to bless, and save us all from Satan's power. And when we come to death's dread hour, Loving Sister Brigid, come and call us to our heavenly home.

PRAYERS TO BLESSED IGNATIUS EDMOND RICE

*Prayer to Blessed Edmond Rice*
Most Holy Trinity, we give you thanks for the life and work of Blessed Edmond Rice. We thank you for the strength and zeal which he placed entirely at your service. We thank you for his outstanding spirit of love and devotion to the poor, and ideal which allowed him no rest until he found the means to help them in body, spirit and mind. His charisma which led him to found the Presentation Order and the Irish Christian Brothers. A spirit which brought thousands of persons of different nations to the true devotion and practice of the faith. Most Holy Trinity we adore you and we beseech you that through the intercession of Blessed Edmond Rice, your servant, we shall have a new outpouring of the Holy Spirit in our Church for the greater glory of God and his son Jesus Christ.

*Prayer to Blessed Edmond Rice for a Favour*
Eternal Father I thank you for the grace you gave to your servant Blessed Edmond Rice of striving to live always in the joy of your presence. For the radiant charity infused into his heart by your Holy Spirit. For the strength he drew from the bread of life to labour for the glory of your name in the care of the young people of Waterford. Confident O Merciful Father that his life was pleasing to you, I beg you grant me through his intercession the special favour I now implore … and make know by miracles the glory he enjoys in heaven. So that he may be glorified through Christ Our Lord. Amen.

## Old Irish Prayers Translated

PRAYER BEFORE MASS
Hail to you, O altar,
O beautiful, flowering, green cross,
let not my soul pass you by.
May you keep in the state of grace,
may you convert us to the right way,
may you enlarge our hearts to be filled with glory,
may you fill our eyes with tears of repentance,
may you give us our share of every Mass
that is celebrated in Rome today
and throughout the whole world. Amen.


PRAYER BEFORE MASS
Blessed are you, O Queen of the Angels,
Blessed are you, O Queen of Glory,
Blessed are you, O Ruler of the Holy Ghost.

The fruit and benefit of this Mass, and of every Mass
that is being said throughout the world, may you give
to us and your fellow creature.

Welcome in our midst, o priest, messenger of God on earth, in your golden vestments and your armour.


PRAYER OF THANKS

Dear God of generosity and Father of graces, who of your free will was tortured and put to death, O Only Son who saved us from sin and from death, relieve the poor Irish and help them in their need.


A PRAYER TO THE HOLY TRINITY

Be you praised a thousand times now, O Father and Lamb; great and loving glory a thousand times over to the Son of God of victories; a thousand times honour, glory and praise to the Surpassing Fruit of creation, the Father, the Son and Holy Ghost, until the grey day of judgment.


A PRAYER FOR GUIDANCE

O Jesus, cleanse my heart in perfect purity every day, O Jesus, put my mind under the full sway of your love. Make my thoughts truly pure and the words of my mouth, and O Lord, dearest God, guide always my life.

A hundred welcomes to thee, O King of Blessed Sunday who has come to help us after the week. My feet guide early to Mass, part of my lips with blessed words, stir up my heart and banish out of it all spite. I look up to the son of the Nurse, her one and only son of mercy, for he it is who has so excellently redeemed us and his we are whether we live or die.

A hundred welcomes to you, O King of Sunday. O Son of the Virgin and King of Glory, O Sweet Jesus, O Son of Mary, have mercy on us.

The King of the Universe is the supreme choice, no help can be compared to mercy, there is no everlasting life save heaven, more previous than anything is the hearing of Mass.


Prayer on our way to Mass
We praise Jesus Christ,
we praise the glorious Sacrament of the altar.
Hail to you, O Mass stone,
hail to you, O blessed Sunday.
Hail to you, O poor crucified Rider
– at your foot we will be saved.

May God and Mary, the Blessed Sacrament
and the priest be at our right hand on our last day.


PRAYER ON ENTERING THE CHURCH
Blessed is the House of God
and I myself greet him
where he is with the twelve apostles.
May the Son of God bless us,
Blessed are you, O Holy Father,
Blessed are you, O Temple of the Holy Ghost,
Blesses are you, O Church of the Trinity.


A PRAYER FOR MERCY
O God of mercy, it was not enough for you to teach us
through your prophets nor through your holy apostles
however faithful their love, but you spoke to us through
Jesus, through the Only Son of Graces who was born of
the Virgin Mary and suffered the Passion, who lived in
our midst and was crucified on the tree to save us from
the punishment of the crime of Eve and Adam.


THE CREED
Lord, completely I believe the sum total of all that with
joy the holy, pure, true and one Catholic Roman Church

founded by Christ firmly believes and holds. And particularly everything that is named specifically from of old in the Creed of the gentle apostles. I yield complete belief, because in your lifetime long ago you really and with full certitude revealed them to us. Every moment of my life I believe unshakably in my heart in one God in three persons, the bright eternal Father, the Most Holy Son of Peace, the Holy Ghost who from them both came.

ACT OF FAITH

I offer up my soul to you, O King of Graces, and may you never permit me to go back on that. Bear witness to this, O Blessed Virgin, that I have put my soul in your son's hands; O Countenance brighter than the sun, suffer me not long to rest in pain.

A thousand welcomes, O Child born in the stable, a warm welcome to your mother's son.

PRAYER AFTER HOLY COMMUNION

A thousand welcomes, O Body of the Lord, you are with me now; purify the place in which you are, expel the root of sin; and O Glorious Virgin be with me.

You are with me now, may you remain with me forever! O heaven on earth, goodness and great health (salvation) may you bring to my soul. Sweet Jesus, my great love, I put the protection of my soul on your right hand now and at the hour of my death, lest in my last hour cannot do so.

A lasting, kindly fitting welcome, Lord. Welcome to you as the incoming tide. Our welcome is like that of the father for his child still in the womb. A welcome to you never to leave us, but to stay forever with us.

PRAYER AFTER HOLY COMMUNION

Hail, Body of Christ, hail King of Wonders, hail Holy Trinity, hail Justice of all Justice. Hail King of Graces, hail Blood and Flesh, O Holy Trinity, without beginning without end, be not angry any more with me. Be not angry anymore with me, wash my soul in the blood of your grace. O God-Man, a hundred welcomes now and at the hour of our death.

PRAYER ON LEAVING THE CHURCH

A thousand welcomes, O noble Jesus, the Lord who suffered for us the Passion and through his side by the sharp spear passed till blood and water flowed out. O Jesus, Son of Mary, have mercy on us.

Farewell Mary, farewell Christ, may you guard our soul till we come back. Farewell, House of God and may God's blessings be about us; may the grace of God not part from us until we return to his church.


### PRAYER BEFORE CONFESSION

O Jesus who put efficacy in the Sacrament, may you fill my heart with God's grace. You granted forgiveness to the thousands you saved. May you save my soul from every sin I have committed.


### PRAYER BEFORE COMMUNION

A hundred thousand welcome, thou Body of the Lord, thou son of her the Virgin, the brightest, most adored. thy death in such fashion on the tree of the Passion hath saved Eve's race and put sin to death.


### PRAYER TO OUR FATHER

Our Father, who are in heaven who fashioned us in the beginning, may your name be made holy and may we all enter your house, your holy and only will may we do it on earth as does everyone in heaven who enters in. The bright bread you made for us, give us, and all our sins may you yourself forgive as the Son forgave the men of the sightless eyes. Let us not go into that kingdom whence there is no return, no, nor into any evil thing nor into the fearsome fires, but amen, O Christ, do you admit us all.

PRAYERS TO THE SACRED HEART
Light of my heart thy Heart, dear Lord, divine,
My treasure bright thy Heart to keep in mine,
Since thy Heart filled, dear Lord, with love for me,
Let mine be a cloak to fold and comfort thee.

Jesus, dear heart, my tongue is no throne for you nor is my heart fit lodging. Only give me your holiness (grace) and may it ever remain with me.

PRAYER BEFORE COMMUNION
Dear Father, who bought us and who art like the sun on the sea, may you forgive us every sin we have ever committed until this day. In heaven, O God, may you forgive our crime so that we may with delight receive Our Lord today.

PRAYER BEFORE COMMUNION

O God, charity without limit and mercy without measure, it is your love that causes you to come to me and it is my hope that brings me to receive you. I give you my body as a temple, my heart as an altar and my soul as a pyx. O Lord, innocent Lamb, Redeemer of Mercy, noble Child, Jesus, cover me with your mantle, give me the lodging in your Heart, envelope me in your kingdom; cure me with your fragrance and charity; enliven me by your death; hide me in your wounds; cleanse me with your blood; bind me with your love and make me utterly pleasing, according to your holy heart, Lord.

PRAYER FOR FORGIVENESS

I am a poor sinner to thee appealing,
Reward me not as my sins may 'be'
O Jesus Christ I deserve thy anger,
But turn again and show grace to me.

Jesus who bought us,
Jesus who taught us,
Jesus of the united prayer, (i.e. the Rosary)
Do not forget us.
Now, nor in the hour of death.

O Crucified Jesus, do not leave us,
thou pouredest thy blood for us, O forgive us,
May the grace of the Spirit forever be with us.
And whatever we ask may the Son of God give us
(Translated by Douglous Hyde)


PRAYER IN HONOUR OF OUR LORDS PASSION
Health to the Noble Son who spread his arms on the tree
of the Passion to free us, and health to the gentle woman
who without man gave birth to her son, and health to
Saint Patrick who blessed Ireland.


PRAYER TO ST MICHAEL
Blessed Michael, archangel, be our safeguard against the
wickedness and snares of the devil. May God restrain
him, we humbly pray; and do thou, O Prince of the
Heavenly Host, by the power of God, thrust Satan down
to hell, and, with him, the other wicked spirits who
wander through the world for the ruin of souls.

V. Most Sacred Heart of Jesus.
R. Have mercy on us. (three times)

# *Hymns*

THOUGH THE MOUNTAINS MAY FALL
Though the mountains may fall
and the hills turn to dust
yet the love of the Lord will stand
As a shelter for all who will call
on his name.
Sing the praise and the glory of God.

Could the Lord ever leave you?
Could the Lord forget his love?
Though a mother forsake her child,
He will not abandon you.

Should you turn and forsake him.
He will gently call your name.
Should you wander away from him,
He will always take you back.

Go to him when you're weary;
He will give you eagle's wings.
You will run, never tire,
For your God will be your strength.

As He swore to your fathers,
when the flood destroyed the land.
He will never forsake you;
He will swear to you again.


FAITH OF OUR FATHERS

1.      Faith of our fathers,
living still in spite of dungeon, fire and sword;
Oh, how our hearts beat high with joy
When e'er we hear that glorious word!

Chorus: Faith of our fathers! Holy Faith!
We will be true to thee till death,
We will be true to thee till death.

2.      Our father, chained in prisons dark,
Were still in heart and conscious free;
How sweet would be their children's fate,
if they like them, could die for thee! (Chorus)

3.      Faith of our fathers, we will love
both friend and foe in all our strife,
and preach thee too, as love knows how,
by kindly words and virtuous life. (Chorus)
(By Frederick William Faber)

HAIL REDEEMER KING DIVINE

1.       Hail, Redeemer, King Divine!
        Priest and Lamb, the throne is thine,
        King, whose reign shall never cease,
        Prince of everlasting peace.

Chorus:  Angels, saints and nations sing;
         'Praised be Jesus Christ, Our King;
         Lord of life, earth, sky and sea,
         King of Love on Calvary!'

2.       King whose name creation thrills,
        rule our minds, our hearts, our wills,
        till in peace each nation rings
        with thy praises, King of Kings. (Chorus)

3.       Eucharistic King, what love
        draws thee daily from above,
        Clad in signs of bread and wine,
        feed us, lead us, keep us thine. (Chorus)
        (By Patrick Brennan CSsR)


SOUL OF MY SAVIOUR

1.       Soul of my Saviour, sanctify my breast;
        Body of Christ, be thou my saving guest;
        Blood of my Saviour, bathe me in thy tide,
        wash me in waters flowing from his side.

2.    Strength and protection may thy Passion be;
      O Blessed Jesus, hear and answer me;
      deep in thy wounds, Lord, hide and shelter me;
      so shall I never, never part from thee.
3.    Guard and defend me from the foe malign;
      in death's dread moments make me only thine;
      call me and bid me come to thee on high
      where I may praise thee with thy saints forever.
      (Ascribed to John XXII/tr. Anonymous)


MY GOD IS MY LOVE
My God is my Love, my Guard from above,
My bright love, my Lord most holy,
My sweet love is Christ, his Heart my delight,
My whole Love, great King of Glory.
My Love, thy soft eye, thy walk is my joy,
My love is thy name and power,
My strong love thou art, though I've wondered apart,
And sinned in an evil hour.


QUEEN OF HEAVEN
My love every day thy word and thy way,
And thy mother, like star beholden,
The Apostles' bright Queen and the angel's unseen

The Queen of the Heavens golden,
The Queen of all light, of happiness bright,
The Queen of the Cross and glory,
O bright Queen of Grace, when grim death I face,
Still aid me, though say my story.


LOVE IS A SHIELD
My love are all those thy bright courts enclose,
My love thy bright form and features,
My love is thy flock who at earth's riches mock,
My love thy great love for thy creatures.
thy Person has sought us, thy Passion has brought us.
In thy city of joy reward us.
O, Christ! Do not yield to thy justice, but shield
thy sinner in need, and guard us.

# *Praying from the Book of Psalms*

PSALM 8 GOD'S GLORY AND MAN'S DIGNITY

O Lord, Our Lord, your greatness is seen in all the world! Your praise reaches up to the heavens;

it is sung by children and babies. You are safe and secure from all your enemies; you stop anyone who opposes you.

When I look at the sky, which you have made, at the moon and the stars, which you set in their places

what is man, that you think of him; mere man, that you care for him?

Yet you made him inferior only to yourself; you crowned him with glory and honour.

You appointed as ruler over everything you made; you placed him ruler over all creation;

sheep and cattle, and the wild animals too;

the birds and the fish and the creatures in the seas.

O Lord, Our Lord, your greatness is seen in all the world!

PSALM 15 What God Requires

Lord, who may enter your Temple? Who may worship
on Zion, your sacred hill?
A person who obeys God in everything and always
does what is right, whose words are true and sincere,
and who does not slander others. He does no wrong to
his friends nor spreads rumours about his neighbours.
He despises those who God rejects, but honours those
who obey the Lord, he always does what he promises,
no matter how it may cost.
He makes loans without charging interest and cannot
be bribed to testify against the innocent. Whoever
does these things will always be secure.


PSALM 67 A Song of Thanksgiving

God, be merciful to us and bless us; look on us with
kindness,
so that the whole world may know your will; so that
all nations may know your salvation.
May the peoples praise you, O God; may all the
peoples praise you!
May the nations be glad and sing for joy, because you
judge the peoples with justice and guide every nation
on earth.

May the peoples praise you, O God; may all the
peoples praise you!
The land has produced its harvest; God, Our God has
blessed us.
God has blessed us; may all the people everywhere
honour him.


PSALM 82 GOD THE SUPREME RULER
God presides in the heavenly council; in the assembly
of the gods he gives his decision:
You must stop judging unjustly; you must no longer
be partial to the wicked!
Defend the rights of the poor and the orphans; be fair
to the needy and the helpless.
Rescue them from the power of evil men.
How ignorant you are! How stupid! You are
completely corrupt, and justice has disappeared from
the world.
'You are gods,' I said, 'all of you are sons of the Most
High. But you will die like men; your life will end like
that of any prince.'
Come, O God, and rule the world, all nations are
yours.

PSALM 93 GOD THE KING

The Lord is king. He is clothed with majesty and strength. The earth is set firmly in place and cannot be moved.

Your throne, O Lord, has been firm from the beginning, and you existed before time began.

The ocean depths raise their voice, O Lord; they raise their voice and roar.

The Lord rules supreme in heaven, greater than the roar of the ocean, more powerful than the waves of the sea.

Your laws are eternal, Lord, and your Temple is holy indeed, forever and ever.


PSALM 131 A PRAYER OF HUMBLE TRUST

Lord, I have given up my pride and turned away from my arrogance. I am not concerned with great matters or with subjects too difficult for me.

Instead, I am content and at peace. As a child lies quietly in its mother's arms.

Israel, trust in the Lord now and forever!

PSALM 133 IN PRAISE OF BROTHERLY LOVE
How wonderful it is, how pleasant,
for God's people to live together in harmony!
It is like the precious anointing oil
running down from Aaron's head and beard,
down to the collar of his robes.
It is like the dew on Mount Hermon,
falling on the hills of Zion.
That is where the Lord has promised his blessing
life that never ends.


PSALM 145 A HYMN OF PRAISE
I will proclaim your greatness,
my God and king;
I will thank you forever and ever.
Every day I will thank you;
I will praise you forever and ever.
The Lord is great and is to be highly praised;
his greatness is beyond understanding.

What you have done will be praised
from one generation to the next;
they will proclaim your mighty acts.
They will speak of your glory and majesty,
and I will meditate on your wonderful deeds.
People will speak of your mighty deeds,

and I will proclaim your greatness.
They will tell all about your goodness
and sing about your kindness.
The Lord is loving and merciful,
slow to become angry and full of constant love.
He is good to everyone
and has compassion on all he made.

All your creatures, Lord, will praise you,
and all your people will give you thanks.
They will speak of the glory of your royal power
and tell of your might,
so that everyone will know your mighty deeds
and the glorious majesty of your kingdom.
Your rule is eternal,
and you are king forever.

The Lord is faithful to his promise,
and he is merciful in all his acts.
He helps those who are in trouble;
he lifts those who have fallen.

All living things look hopefully to you,
and you give them food when
they need it.
You give them enough
and satisfy the needs of all.

The Lord is righteous in all he does,
merciful in all his acts.
He is near to those who call to him, who call to him
with sincerity.
He supplies the needs of those who honour him;
he hears their cries and saves them.
He protects everyone who loves him,
but he will destroy the wicked.

I will always praise the Lord;
Let all his creatures praise his holy
name forever.


PSALM 98 GOD THE RULER OF THE WORLD
Sing a new song to the Lord;
he has done wonderful things!
By his own power and holy strength
he has won the victory.
The Lord announced his victory;
he made his savings power known to the nations.
He kept his promises to the people of Israel
with loyalty and constant love for them.
All people everywhere have seen the victory of Our
God.

Sing for joy to the Lord, all the earth;
praise him with songs and shouts of joy!
Sing praises to the Lord!
Play music on the harps!
Blow trumpets and horns,
and shout for joy to the Lord, our king.

Roar, sea, and every creature in you;
sing, earth, and all who live on you!
Clap your hands, your rivers;
your hills, sing together with joy before the Lord,
because he comes to rule the earth.
He will rule the peoples of the world
with justice and fairness.

PSALM 100 A HYMN OF PRAISE
Sing to the Lord, all the world!
Worship the Lord with joy;
come before him with happy songs!
Acknowledge that the Lord is God.
He made us, and we belong to him;
we are his people, we are his flock.
Enter the temple gates with thanksgiving,
go into its courts with praise.
Give thanks to him and praise him.

The Lord is good;
his love is eternal
and his faithfulness lasts forever.

PSALM 117 IN PRAISE OF THE LORD
Praise the Lord, all nations!
Praise him, all peoples!
His love for us is strong
and his faithfulness is eternal.
Praise the Lord!

PSALM 121 THE LORD OUR PROTECTOR
I look to the mountains;
where will my help come from.
My help will come from the Lord,
who made heaven and earth.

He will not let you fall;
your protector is always awake.

The protector of Israel
never dozes or sleeps.
The Lord will guard you;
he is by your side to protect you.

The sun will not hurt you during the day,
nor the moon during the night.

The Lord will protect you from all danger;
he will keep you safe.
He will protect you as you come and go
now and forever.


PSALM 123 A Prayer for Mercy
Lord, I look up to you,
up to heaven, where you rule,
As a servant depends on his master,
as a maid depends on her mistress,
so we will keep looking to you, O Lord Our God,
until you have mercy on us.

Be merciful to us, Lord, be merciful;
we have been treated with so much contempt.
We have been mocked too long by the rich
and scorned by proud oppressors.


PSALM 126 A Prayer for Deliverance
When the Lord brought us back to Jerusalem,
it was like a dream!
How we laughed, how we sang for joy!

Then the other nations said about us,
'The Lord did great things for them'
Indeed he did great things for us;
how happy we were!

Lord, make us prosperous again,
just as the rain brings water back to dry riverbeds.
Let those who wept as they sowed their seed,
gather the harvest with joy!

Those who wept as they went out
carrying the seed
will come back singing for joy,
as they bring in the harvest.


PSALM 127 In Praise of God's Goodness
If the Lord does not build the house,
the work of the builders is useless;
if the Lord does not protect the city
it is useless for the sentries to stand guard.
It is useless to work so hard for a living,
getting up early and going to bed late.
For the Lord provides for those he loves,
while they are asleep.

Children are a gift from the Lord;
they are a real blessing.

The sons a man has when he is young
are like arrows in a soldier's hand.
Happy is the man who has many such arrows.
He will never be defeated
when he meets enemies in the place of judgment.


PSALM 30 A PRAYER FOR HELP
From the depths of my despair
I call to you, Lord.
Hear my cry, O Lord;
listen to my call for help!
If you could keep a record of our sins,
who could escape being condemned,
But you forgive us,
so that we should stand in awe of you.

I wait eagerly for the Lord's help,
and in his word I trust.
I wait for the Lord
more eagerly than watchmen wait for the dawn.

Israel, trust in the Lord,
because his love is constant
and he is always willing to save.
He will save his people Israel from all their sins.

# Scripture Verses from the Word of God

HOSEA 4:1–3

Hear the Word of the Lord, O people; for the Lord has a controversy with the inhabitants of the land. There is no faithfulness or kindness, and no knowledge of God in the land; there is swearing, lying, killing and committing adultery; they break all bounds and murder follows murder. Therefore the land mourns, and all who dwell in it languish, and also the beasts of the air; and even the fish of the sea are taken away.

ISAIAH 55:6–11

Seek the Lord while he may be found, call upon him while he is near; let the wicked forsake his way, and the unrighteous man his thoughts; let him return to the Lord, that he may have mercy on him, and to Our God, for he will abundantly pardon. For my thoughts are not your thoughts, neither are your ways my ways, says the Lord. For as the heavens are higher than the earth, so are my ways higher than your ways, and my thoughts than your thoughts. For as the rain and the snow come down from heaven, and return no thither but water the earth, making it bring forth and sprout, giving seed to the sower and bread to the eater, so shall my word be that goes forth from my mouth; it shall not return to me empty, but it shall accomplish that which I purpose and prosper in the thing for which I sent it.

EXODUS 20:6–11
Remember the Sabbath day, to keep it holy. Six days you shall labour, and do all your work; but the seventh day is a Sabbath to the Lord your God; in it you shall not do any work, you or your son, or your daughter, your manservant or your maid-servant, or your cattle, or the sojourner who is within your gates. For in six days the Lord made heaven and earth, the sea and all that is in them and rested the seventh day, therefore the Lord blessed the Sabbath day and hallowed it.

PETER 2:1–6
So put away all malice and all guilt and insincerity and envy all slander. Like newborn babies, long for the pure spiritual milk, that by it you may grow up to salvation; for you have tasted the kindness of the Lord. Come to

him, to that living stone, rejected by men in God's sight chosen and precious; and like living stones be yourselves built into a spiritual house, to be a holy priesthood, to offer spiritual sacrifices acceptable to God through Jesus Christ. For it stands in scripture.

Isaiah 11:1–9
There shall come forth a shoot from the stump of Jesse and a branch shall grow out of his roots. And the Spirit of the Lord shall rest upon him, the spirit of counsel and might, the spirit of knowledge and the fear of the Lord. And his delight shall be in the fear of the Lord. He shall not judge what his eyes see, or decide by what his ears hear; but with righteousness he shall judge the poor, and decided with equity for the meek of the earth; and he shall smite the earth with the rod of his mouth, and with the breath of his lips he shall slay the wicked. Righteousness shall be the girdle of his waist, and faithfulness the girdle of his loins.

The wolf shall dwell with the lamb, and the leopard shall lie down with the kid, and the calf and the lion and the fatling together, and a little child shall lead them. The cow and the bear shall feed; their young shall lie down together; and the lion shall eat straw like the ox. The sucking child shall play over the hole of the asp, and the weaned child shall put his hand on the adder's den. They shall not hurt or destroy in all my holy mountain; for the earth shall be full of the knowledge of the Lord, as the waters cover the sea.

DEUTERONOMY 32:1–10

Give ear, O heavens, and I will speak; and let the earth hear the words of my mouth. May my teaching drop as the rain, my speech be still as the dew, as the gentle rain upon the tender grass, and as the showers upon the herb. For I will proclaim the name of the Lord. Ascribe greatness to Our God!

The Rock, his work is perfect; for all his ways are justice. A God of faithfulness and without iniquity, just and right is he. They have dealt corruptly with him, they are no longer his children because of their blemish, they are a perverse and crooked generation. Do you thus requite the Lord, you foolish and senseless people. Is not he your father, who created you, who made you and established you. Remember the days of old, consider the years of many generations; ask your father, and he will show you; your elders, and they will tell you. When the Most High gave to the nations their inheritance, when he separated the sons of men, he fixed the bounds of the peoples according to the number of the sons of God, For the Lord's portion is his people, Jacob his allotted heritage. He found him in a desert land, and in the howling waste of the wilderness; he encircled him, he cared for him, he kept him as the apple of his eye.

EPHESIANS 6:10–20
Be strong in the Lord and in the strength of his might. Put on the whole armour of God, that you may be able to stand out against the wiles of the devil. For we are not contending against flesh and blood, but against the principalities, against the powers, against the world rules of this present darkness, against the spiritual hosts of wickedness in the heavenly places. Therefore take the whole armour of God, that you may be able to withstand in the evil day, and having done all, stand there for having girded your lions with truth, and having put on the breastplate of righteousness, and having shod your feet with the equipment of the gospel of peace; above all taking the shield of faith, with which you can quench all the flaming darts of the evil one. And take the helmet of salvation, and the sword of the Spirit, which is the Word of God. Pray at all times in the Spirit, with all prayer and supplication. To that end keep alert with all perseverance, making supplication for all the saints, and also for me, that utterance may be given me

in opening my mouth boldly to proclaim the mystery of the gospel, for which I am an ambassador in chains; that I may declare it boldly, as I ought to speak.

MATTHEW 7:1–5
Judge not, that you be not judged. For with the judgment you pronounce you will be judged, and the measure you will give will be the measure you get. Why do you see the speck that is in your brother's eye, but do not notice the log that is in your own eye. You hypocrite, first take the log out of your own eye and then you will see clearly to take the speck out of your brothers eye.

MATTHEW 7:7–12
Ask and it will be given to you; seek and you will find; knock, and it will be opened to you. For every one who asks receives, and he who seeks finds, and to him who knocks it will be opened. Or what man of you, if his son asks him for bread, will give him a stone. Or if he asks for a fish, will you give him a serpent. If you then, who are evil, know how to give good gifts to your children, how much more will your Father who is in heaven give good things to those who ask him. So whatever you

wish that men would do to you, do so to them; for this is the law and the prophets.

## MATTHEW 6:25–34

Therefore I tell you, do not be anxious about your life, what you shall eat or what you shall drink, nor about your body, what you shall put on. Is not life more than food, and the body more than clothing. Look at the birds of the air; they neither sow nor reap nor gather into barns, and yet your heavenly Father feeds them. Are you not of more value than they. And which of you by being anxious can add one cubit to his span of life. And why are you anxious about clothing. Consider the lilies of the field, how they grow; they neither toil nor spin; yet I tell you, even Solomon in all his glory was not arrayed like one of these. But if God so clothes the grass in the field, which today is alive and tomorrow is thrown into the oven, will he not much more clothe you. O men of little faith. Therefore do not be anxious, saying 'what shall we eat' or 'what shall we drink' or 'what shall we wear'. For the Gentiles seek all these things; and your heavenly Father knows that you need them all. But seek first his kingdom and his righteousness, and all these things shall be yours as well. Therefore do not be anxious about tomorrow, for tomorrow will be anxious for itself. Let the day's own trouble be sufficient for the day.

MATTHEW 13:44–52
The kingdom of heaven is like treasure hidden in a field, which a man found and covered up then in his joy he goes and sells all that he has and buys that field. Again, the kingdom of heaven is like a merchant in search of fine pearls, who, on finding one pearl of great value went and sold all that he had and bought it. Again, the kingdom of heaven is like a net which was thrown into the sea and gathered fish of every king; when it was full, men drew it ashore and sat down and sorted the good into vessels but threw away the bad. So it will be at the close of the age. The angels will come out and separate the evil from the righteous, and throw them into the furnace of fire; there men will weep and gnash their teeth. 'Have you understood all this?' they said to him. 'Yes.' And he said to them, 'Therefore every scribe who has been trained for the kingdom of heaven is like a householder who brings out of his treasure what is new and what is old.'

EPHESIANS 2:1–9; 19–22

And you are made alive, when you were dead through the trespasses and sins, in which you once walked, following the course of this world, following the Prince of Power of the air, the spirit that is now at work in the sons of disobedience, among these we all once lived in the passions of our flesh, following the desires of body and mind, and so we were by nature children of wrath like the rest of mankind. But God who is rich in mercy, out of the great love with which he loved us, even when we are dead through our trespasses, made us alive together with Christ. By grace you have been saved, and he raised us up with him, and made us sit with him in the heavenly places in Jesus Christ, that in the coming ages he might show the riches of his grace in kindness towards us in Christ Jesus. For by grace you have been saved through faith. This is the gift of God.

So then you are no longer strangers and sojourners, but you are fellow citizens with the saints and members of the Household of God. Built upon the Foundation of the apostles and prophets, Christ Jesus himself being the Cornerstone in whom the whole structure is joined together and grows into a holy temple in the Lord, in whom you also are built into it for a swelling place of God in the Spirit.

REVELATIONS 21:3–6

Behold, the dwelling of God is with men. He will dwell with them, and they shall be his people, and God himself will be with them; he will wipe away every tear from their eyes, and death shall be no more, neither shall there be mourning nor crying nor pain any more, for the former things have passed away. As he who sat upon the throne said, 'Behold, I make all things new.' Also he said, 'Write this, for these words, are trustworthy and true.' And he said to me, 'It is done! I am the Alpha and the Omega, the beginning and the end.'

# The Church's Teaching

THE TEN COMMANDMENTS OF GOD

1.  Thou shalt not have strange gods before me. Thou shalt not make to thyself any graven thing; nor the likeness of anything that is in heaven above, or in earth beneath, nor of those things that are in the waters under the earth. Thou shall not adore them or serve them.

2.  Thou shalt not take the name of the Lord thy God in vain.

3.  Remember that thou keep holy the Sabbath day.

4.  Honour thy father and thy mother.

5.  Thou shalt not kill.

6.  Thou shalt not commit adultery.

7.  Thou shalt not steal.

8.  Thou shalt not bear false witness against thy neighbour.

9.  Thou shalt not covet they neighbour's wife.

10. Thou shalt not covet thy neighbour's goods.

THE SIX CHIEF COMMANDMENTS OF THE CHURCH

1.  To keep the Sundays and holy days of Obligation
    holy, by hearing Mass and resting from servile
    works.

2.  To keep the days of Fasting and Abstinence
    appointed by the Church.

3.  To go to confession at least once a year.

4.  To receive the Blessed Sacrament at least once a
    year, at Easter or thereabouts.

5.  To contribute to the support of our pastors.

6.  Not to marry within certain degrees of kindred
    without dispensation.


THE SEVEN SACRAMENTS

*1. Baptism*

By which we are made Christians, children of God,
members of his holy Church, and heirs of heaven.

*2. Confirmation*

By which we receive the Holy Spirit, to make us strong
and perfect Christians, and soldiers of Christ.

*3. The Holy Eucharist*

Which is really and truly and substantially the Body and

Blood, the Soul and Divinity, of Jesus Christ, under the appearances of bread and wine. The Holy Eucharist is not only a Sacrament, in which we receive our divine Lord for the food and nourishment of our souls, and in which he is really present to be adored upon the altar; it is also a sacrifice, the Sacrifice of Holy Mass, in which, at the time of consecration, the bread and wine are changed into the Body and Blood of Jesus Christ, and in which he is offered up for us to his eternal Father.

### 4. *Penance*
By which the sins committed after Baptism are forgiven.

### 5. *Anointing of the Sick*
Which, in dangerous illness, and in preparation for death, comforts the soul, remits sin, and restores health if God sees this to be expedient.

### 6. *Holy Order*
By which bishops, priests, and other ministers of the Church receive power and grace to perform their sacred duties.

### 7. *Matrimony*
Which is the Sacrament of Christian Marriage.

## THE THREE THEOLOGICAL VIRTUES

- ❖ Faith
- ❖ Hope
- ❖ Charity

## THE FOUR CARDINAL VIRTUES

- ❖ Prudence
- ❖ Justice
- ❖ Fortitude
- ❖ Temperance

## THE SEVEN GIFTS OF THE HOLY SPIRIT

- ❖ Wisdom
- ❖ Counsel
- ❖ Knowledge
- ❖ Fortitude
- ❖ Understanding
- ❖ The Fear of the Lord
- ❖ Piety

## THE TWELVE FRUITS OF THE HOLY SPIRIT

- ❖ Charity
- ❖ Self control
- ❖ Joy
- ❖ Goodness
- ❖ Peace
- ❖ Generosity

| ❖ Mildness | ❖ Faith | ❖ Modesty |
| ❖ Faithfulness | ❖ Chastity | ❖ Patience |

## THE SEVEN CORPORAL WORKS OF MERCY

- ❖ To feed the hungry
- ❖ To harbour the harbourless
- ❖ To give drink to the thirsty
- ❖ To visit the sick
- ❖ To clothe the naked
- ❖ To visit the imprisoned
- ❖ To bury the dead

## THE SEVEN SPIRITUAL WORKS OF MERCY

- ❖ To counsel the doubtful
- ❖ To instruct the ignorant
- ❖ To admonish the sinners
- ❖ To comfort the afflicted
- ❖ To forgive offences
- ❖ To bear wrongs patiently
- ❖ To pray for the living and the dead

## The Seven Deadly Sins

- Pride
- Lust
- Gluttony
- Sloth
- Covetousness
- Anger
- Envy

## The Opposite Virtues

- Humility
- Chastity
- Temperance
- Diligence
- Liberality
- Meekness
- Brotherly Love

## *Like A Shepherd*

Like a shepherd he feeds his flock,
And gathers the lambs in his arms,
Holding them carefully close to his heart,
Leading them home.
Say to the cities of Judah:
Prepare the way of the Lord.
Go to the mountaintop, lift your voice;
Jerusalem, here is your God.
I myself will shepherd them,
For others have led them astray.
The lost I will rescue and heal their wounds,
And pasture them, giving them rest.
Come unto me,
If you are heavily burdened,
And take my yoke upon your shoulders,
I will give you rest.

# Our Lord's Last Promise

Let not your heart be troubled.
You believe in God,
believe also in me.
In my Father's house
there are many mansions.
If not, I would have told you;
Because I go to prepare
a place for you.
I will come again,
and will take you to myself;
That where I am, you also may be.
And whither I go you know,
and the way you know.
I am the way and the truth,
and the life.